Homecoming

Acknowledgements

Thanks are due to the editors of the following publications, where some of these poems, or earlier versions of then, first appeared: *Entanglements: New Eco-Poetry* (Two Ravens Press); *The Sheffield Anthology: Poems from the City Imagined*(smith|doorstop); *The Captain's Tower: Seventy Poets for Bob Dylan's 70th Birthday* (Seren); *From Childhood's Hour* (Ledbury Poetry Festival); *Sculpted* (North West Poets); *Not On Our Green Belt* (North West Poets); *The Reader*.

A number of these poems appeared as a limited edition pamphlet, 'Digging', illustrated by Hugh Bryden and published by Roncadora Press in 2010. Thanks are also due once again to Hugh Bryden for his wonderful cover art.

'Lindale Hill' was commissioned by Cumbria County Council Library Service for its Reading Detectives project in 2010.

The second stanza of 'April in Town End', was produced as a poster and postcard by North West Libraries' Time to Read as part of their Perfect Places project in 2012, as 'April in Dove Cottage'.

'Grasmere Green: Summer Equinox' was written for 'Solstice', a project devised and edited by Sarah Hymas & Rebecca Bilkau.

The author is grateful to Hawthornden International Retreat for Writers for a Fellowship in 2012 which gave the valuable gift of time to write a number of these poems and to shape this collection. Thanks are due also to Michael McGregor and the Wordsworth Trust for supporting this Fellowship.

The author would like to acknowledge the financial support of a New Writing North Northern Writers Award supported by Northumbria University and Arts Council England.

Special thanks to my friends whose careful insights have made these poems stronger: Carola Luther, Mike Barlow, Anne Caldwell, Rebecca Goss, Helen Mort and Vicki Feaver.

Homecoming
Andrew Forster

smith|doorstop

Published 2014 by
smith|doorstop Books
The Poetry Business
Bank Street Arts
32-40 Bank Street
Sheffield S1 2DS
www.poetrybusiness.co.uk

ISBN 978-1-910367-04-9

British Library Cataloguing-in-Publication Data.
A catalogue record for this book is available from the
British Library.

Typeset by Utter

Cover image: Hugh Bryden
Author photo: Henry Iddon
Printed and bound by CPI Group (UK) Ltd, Croydon, CR0 4YY
smith|doorstop Books is a member of Inpress,
www.inpressbooks.co.uk. Distributed by Central Books Ltd.,
99 Wallis Road, London E9 5LN.

The Poetry Business is an Arts Council
National Portfolio Organisation

Contents

*For Stephen, for putting up with being the
brother in* Brothers!

At Carstairs Junction

On the northbound platform, changing trains
in this village where routes converge,
the darkness hasn't loosened its hold.
Rain slants into the lamps like the grain

of an old film. The waiting room
is small, the platform crammed, commuters
not speaking, trying to read the blackness
beyond the edge of the station.

Tomorrow, my car will hit ice
and I'll crash down the snow-mapped bank.

In the slow days of convalescence, I think
about my days and nights spent travelling
and decide to plot a different course
but this morning I'm locked into this one.

A train draws in behind us, carriages
warm with the glow of home, and perhaps
it's only hindsight that hears the wheels
whisper *south, south* as it pulls away.

Digging

for John Manson

The careful note on the door says *Welcome*
in four languages, but my knock
brings no shuffle of footsteps.
While I wait there's a scrape of steel
on soil from the back garden.

The sun squeezes into the grey wash of sky.
In tracksuit and old dress shoes
he turns earth over in rows.
Always more professor than crofter,
he is out of place in the open air.

His study is a secret chamber:
one small window that doesn't reach the sun,
volumes of MacDiarmid piled into pillars
and a Remington on the desk,
white keys shining in the constant dusk.

Here he sifts the random thoughts of poets
for that sudden glint that draws the eye
like a fragment of a painted vase
in a spadeful of earth. He passes me
a book and we go back to the day.

Clouds are seamed with black. He looks up.
I used to spend each hour I could at my desk
he says but now the light seems more important.
The brief sun catches his thinning hair
as he bends to prepare the ground.

Ullswater

From Patterdale it's a haul up sheep tracks
through a grassy fold. The broken mouth
of a slate mine gawps, half-hidden by a hawthorn,
the hillside almost healed around it.

We're staying at *Seldom Seen*, where a stone
chipped off the track and cracked the car's sump.
While the garage waits for the part, we shelve
our travel plans, forced to stay closer to home.

Above Silver Point, the path drops over
stone steps, recent rains spilling down.
We grab handfuls of grass, place feet against
water's push, sudden wind pulling our clothes.

Near here, the boy Wordsworth stole a boat
and rowed out onto the lake.
Stybarrow Crag rushed towards him and
he suddenly knew how small we all are.

Ullswater stretches to kiss the rock,
colours deepening towards the horizon
from eggshell to cobalt to navy.
Far out, a boat surges in a crosswind.

Bats

They emerge when day has bleached from the sky
through a sliver of space beneath the roof:
two, I think, but they're so fast they vanish
and reappear from somewhere else,
each a shallow wave where they jerk
the membrane that serves for wings,
tiny mouths screaming to map the landscape.

They're bad luck, darkness, *winged rats*
flitting through crowded tenements,
or *flying souls*, our last spark
given form in the dusk as it leaves us.
In Levens a whole colony funneled
between the trees and we stood beneath,
altered by their sudden current.

I remember the dead one on the gravel:
brown fur coarse as wire wool, wings a cape,
face wizened and faintly human,
the oldest man that ever was.
It had dropped from another world, as if
what we see in flight is a privileged glimpse
of something we must fail to understand.

Grasmere: Summer Evening

From the dusty green heights of Silver Howe
the lake is beaten pewter, the island
a universe of rushes in the centre.
Town End's terraces of mountain slate
look like they slid to a halt at the bottom
of a slope, and trees took root in them.

After school, Wordsworth pushed back
the edges of his world on nightly rambles.
He looked into this valley and his mind skittered
over fields and crags like some animal spirit.
He yearned to make a home here
perfectly contained in this bowl of hills.

Down on the shore the lake barely ripples.
It's this stillness that brings us back here,
hills holding their silence beyond the streams
of visitors. At the end of the lane,
deer bask on the grass as the sun relaxes.
They might have been here for centuries.

Lindale Hill

It's a village of layers, a place
in progress, where houses are messages
from different ages: rain-polished slate,
wind-roughened stone, perfect brick
or blues and greys, evenly-painted.

Rock roses cascade from garden walls
like secrets refusing to stay hidden.
In spaces between buildings, beeches
weighed down with ivy, reach from rocks
in gestures that aren't quite translatable.

A double-stemmed chestnut, rusty, flaking,
grows out of gravel where the millpond was.
The wooden board shows drawings
of millworkers' cottages, demolished,
making room for traffic to somewhere else.

Streets branch off, cutting corners,
leading to crossroads or dead-ends.
The millrace is a dry channel beside the beck
blocked with bricks, lined with copper leaves,
leading only to an asphalt carpark.

The beck itself curves over stone lips,
splashing and foaming and muttering
in its own tongue as it runs a broken course,
disappears into tunnels, emerges
only briefly, then returns underground.

Greenhead Ghyll

After bare sun on crags and the sultry stillness
of Alcock Tarn, it's a relief to descend
through bracken as day eases into evening.
Greenhead Ghyll splashes, sweetening the air.

Across it there's a sheepfold: worn by rain
and wind, uneven where stones have worked loose
or sections collapsed, but it's still there, gaps
opening to separate pens, a refuge.

On his walks Wordsworth spoke to shepherds
who scratched a living from thin soil
as their families had: who knew the hills
like rooms in their own cottages.

They watched their children, through choice
or need, leave for the city, and knew
their land must pass to other hands.

He stared at the sheepfold until his head ached,
gave them his poem like a cry for help.
Now, houses clutter the lower slopes
windows drinking in these hills.

A few cars are parked in drives, the odd voice
rides the breeze but most of the houses
are empty. A runner almost knocks me over
as he thunders down the Fell.

Grange-over-Sands

This November Sunday we're the only ones
strolling past the planted border where
an odd splash of red, drying to parchment
at its edge, shines from shingle like an old flag.

The railway runs beside us, cutting in front
of the town. Merchants rode it here but
carriages used to cross the bay, horses stumbling
over fickle sands before the tide could turn.

Now the sea is a distant line and sheep
graze saltmarsh, water reaching us
only through narrow channels shaped
like letters from a forgotten language.

On a bench, a brass plaque remembers
someone else who loved this place. We gaze
across to Morecambe, and can almost see guests
enter the white shimmer of the Midland Hotel.

We should grow old here, in this town
of terraces; merchants' houses matured
to hotels and nursing homes, looking down,
waiting for the sea to change its course back.

Morecambe Bay

It's a glass pathway, leading out;
shining, but scratched
and splintering at the edges.

*

It's a grey muslin sheet, ruffled
in the breeze, lifting at the corners
so the sand can be seen sleeping.

*

It's a blue eiderdown, billowing
around the unconscious turns
of an invisible dreamer.

*

It could be ice, the currents scuffing
the surface like the blades of skaters,
pretending it would hold your weight.

*

It's empty, except for thin trails sparkling
like those of enormous snails,
on sand that mimics being still.

*

It licks at the saltmarsh, filling
channels with ease and confidence,
as if it's always like this.

✳

It's a web of streams and rivers
reflecting the white sun like gossamer
after rain, trembling but holding fast.

✳

It hurls itself against the prom wall,
batters itself into a wet glitter,
surges onto the walkway.

Horses at Castle Head

Snow blankets the grass but still the girl
gives them the field: a black horse, sixteen hands,
the Shetland half that. She pats them before
she leaves, forks hay over the gate, a blast
of yellow on the white ground. Each day,
wrapped in quilted coats, hooves scuff earth
and wind combs their manes. At the back of the field
is a roped track, but these horses are left alone.

They're rarely apart, each the other's shadow.
Children shout as they sledge down the hill
across the road, but the horses pay no mind.
More snow detaches from the darkening sky.
They stay close, breath clouding the air,
listening to something only they can hear.

Wordsworth Skating

Air so cold you could snatch it in handfuls.
Last night, the radio said, temperatures dropped
low as the South Pole, but it's still a surprise
to drive past birches sculpted from frost
and see Rydal Water frozen over:
the islands, with tangles of leafless willow,
locked in like a foxed mirror.

I can see Wordsworth, grey-haired, buttoned tight,
legs splayed, on strap-on blades, oblivious
to de Quincey's sneers of "a cow, dancing".
Eyes watering, a smile on his lips,
he remembers racing across ice
in a nocturnal pack, and stopping
suddenly, to set the dark cliffs spinning.

This morning, the frozen lake sparkles
as the sun pulls itself over Loughrigg
and only a swan occupies the surface,
long neck bending to preen its wings.
At the edge, ice chimes against the rushes,
so delicate a breath would shatter it.

Snow in Lindale

Mossed slates and scuffed gardens are fleeced
with snow. The scratched glass of the frozen stream
curves through the drifts and falls of the field.
Sheep cast long shadows, stand still, as if
they've forgotten where they are. On our lawn,
holes in the snow, too deep for cats' paws:
the night leaving tracks in the day.

❋

The few cars labour, headlights on,
wheels cutting through snow.
I'm two years and a hundred miles south
from when, driving home on the Leadhills road,
I lost purchase on a run of ice
and ploughed down the scrubby bank
towards trees with trunks like iron.

❋

Children waste no time. Bundled in coats,
scarves loose around necks in grudged concession,
they drag sledges to the top of the hill.
The snow's too wet to bear their weight for long,
the bashed-together wood or metal runners
churning it to slush, sledges sputtering
to a stop before they've really picked up speed.

❋

You tell me that, back in Cape Town, rarely,
thin drifts would appear on Table Mountain,
shallow as a fingertip, more frost than snow,
and buses shuttled the adventurous
to Signal Hill. Once, you made a snowman
with seedpods and fragments of stone
for eyes, mouth and nose. 'Nearly six inches high.'

Kentmere Valley

Stone walls own the fields, solid, unarguable,
but few sheep and cattle graze within them.
Barns stand open, quiet, and water troughs
each choked with an ingot of ice.

❋

A mountain of slate looms, remains of a mine,
the winch tower at the back like a fortress.
Grass roots in the jagged layers
pulling it back into the landscape.

❋

The ground underfoot is humped as if
there's a wall or walkway there, the traces
of Anglo-Saxon settlers hidden in the soil,
running like a grid beneath the valley.

❋

Crags steam with mist as if newly-formed,
rise out of broken bracken. High up
a single hawthorn reaches from rock.
The path loses itself in a sea of rushes.

❋

Damp in the air leaves patterns on the skin
as if telling a story beyond language.
The corpse of an ash tree is twisted, perished,
but a poplar has taken root inside it.

＊

The reservoir crowns the valley,
water so still there's no border
between landscape and reflection
and to look down into it, beyond mirrored fells
is to look into emptiness, back to the start.

Standing Water

Driving home is a slow trawl in the dark
through land that's being remade by rain:
the River Rothay has raised its level,
forced into a foaming current, straining
against banks, streaming over shallow channels.

These scenes are more frequent now.
The petrol station on the Kendal by-pass
is a harbour station, pumps
half-drowned, standing in the water
like marker buoys or miracles.

Snakes

They're all over the suburbs in Cape Town, sliding
onto tarmac at night to stretch out on stored heat.
You hunted grass-snakes in gangs, battering bushes
with sticks, trapping them with forked branches.
They're not deadly, but you still stayed at the edge.

Your mother was watering the garden
when a cobra slipped into the sun-warmed coils
of hosepipe. Then, in your own house, your cat
dragged one into the kitchen, the snake
wrapping itself around the cat's legs.

In the Eastern Cape, a labourer was bitten
by a rattler, the farmer sucking out the poison.
There was the puff adder too,
inflating and deflating, hypnotic
as a metronome, hissing like escaping gas.

Even here, years away, where adders on saltmarsh
are rare after two cold winters, sometimes
in sleep your eyelids flicker. Waking one morning,
you said you'd been bitten, my denial no comfort
against the creatures slithering through your night.

Easedale Tarn

Sour Milk Ghyll murmurs the same
old phrases. It inhales sharply then drops
over rocks, shocked at the change of course
but recovering with casual curses.
The path rolls beside it like a carpet.
Wind in long grass picks up the stream's thought.

A Herdwick blocks my way, black
against the failing sun; bred
for these mountains, not easily startled,
grey fleece heavy for the sullen weather.
It dismisses me and springs up the bank.

The tarn is a sheet of glass, blue gathering
strength from the landscape around it.
On the far bank, a tent flaps in the breeze,
and a father and son share the dusk
beside a fire, sticks cracking like gunshots.

I'm careful not to disturb them. Easy to think
little has changed since Wordsworth and his sister
marched up here: he in double-soled shoes,
she with skirts hitched up, most unlike a lady.
They sat and spoke with the Drovers,
hearing stories and confessing their hope
that some people of this Vale, two or three perhaps,
might remember them, after they'd gone.

Swans

I'd seen the pair, gliding along the cut:
the white question mark of their necks,
steep curve of wings at rest, perfect ease
of movement; an existence apart,
their gaze fixed somewhere beyond
the ploughed fields and steep tiers of houses.

The next week, walking to Brigsteer, I turned
a corner and there they were, across the dyke,
on a bare patch of bank, before a hedge
of foaming meadowsweet and hawthorn:
the swans, with seven cygnets beside them,
in full view of passing cars or predators.

Fluffy with grey down, eyes barely open,
each shuffled around its patch of earth
pushing against the limits of movement.
I held back, wary of startling them
but the adults stayed relaxed, shrugging
magnificent wings just once, then settling

into stillness, pride as physical
as heat. I wish that family well.
I wish them safety from prowling foxes
and the casual damage of tractors.
I watch for them, sailing through the summer,
changing the evening with their passing.

On The Waterwitch

The world from a mallard's perspective:
Fields climbing away from us, we putter south
from Crooklands to Millness Culvert,
through duckweed thick as frogspawn,
sun dripping into green water.

Five moorhen chicks race over lilypads
without even tilting them, as if made
entirely from grey down. At our approach
their mother, electric black, beak red
as an alarm bell, herds them into the rushes.

A single swan rests on the far bank,
separate from the canal's rhythms.
Its cygnets test the water, splashing in,
waddling back, each time pushing the edges
of their world that little bit further.

This boat once hauled coal to Cumbria,
returning to the south with slate. Now,
last of its line on this northern stretch
it keeps the day to its own pace
beside fields and roads in the shallow canal.

Three young bulls wade, chewing watermint,
all sculpted muscle, shins seeming too lean
to carry their torsos. As we near, one turns
and steps up the bank, light as a dancer,
shedding water like an old skin.

Elterwater

Climbing Drovers' paths over Silver How,
down limestone gullies beneath a bleached-out sky.
careful not to slip on streams of scree;
Elterwater Village seems here by accident,
gabled cottages and converted barns.
The Lake is merely Tarn, opaque
as old ice, hidden by rushes;
the road is a straight line past to the head
of the valley, for the challenge of the peaks.

Wordsworth came here to fish and lost his line.
Dorothy slept, head on a mossy rock
then started on the wrong path through the woods.
They looked over at the settlement,
clustered against weather and strangers,
which, on this day, struck even them as bleak.
But they'd return: they knew how
to be in a place, those two: how to plunge
into a landscape, take its stories to heart.

Humphrey Head

The last wolf in England was hunted here
where the headland rises, such a dazzling white
that people believed fairies painted it.
Limestone shelves and pillars jut from sand
and in the tenderness of early evening
the path between them feels like a street
in a deserted city. Tiny streams
trickle like rain from broken gutters.

A wolf in flight seems almost to float
which could be why we've made them
shape-shifters, vampires, the very Devil;
but as that wolf moved like floodwater
over fields to Newby Bridge, Coniston Old Man
and down to where Windermere tongued the shore,
could those who saw it feel other
than a longing to race beside it?

Back at last it ran out of land
and waited on the beach for the last hunter,
as still and spent as a dried-out riverbed.
Now, in the hour of long shadows, sheep
don't even pause as I stroll past.
Far out, a child laughs, or cries,
the sound shimmering above the bay.

The Hospice

A folly, lifting out of sheep-cropped grass
at the summit of Hampsfell, a resting place
for monks on the Cistercian Way. Inside
three walls lined with wooden benches,
a fireplace on the fourth like a small cave,
littered by a recent fire. Stone steps
lead to the roof, where a compass
plots and names the landscape, from Skiddaw
down around the bay to Morecambe.

Today the Fell streams with families,
finding their way over limestone outcrops
like old bones. We're not far
from cars, homes and a nearby town
that has grown in the last two centuries.
We all know exactly where we are
but we move the pointer anyway,
checking its accuracy, oak smooth
and reassuring beneath our hands.

Dove Cottage

Set back, between lane and wooded slope,
quiet white letters on a blue sign
stake their claim, and a pink rose climbs
the white pebbledash, its blooms fragile
as parchment and pure as an idea.

Inside, huddles of visitors are guided from
the *house-place* to the *out-jutting*,
trying to glimpse the poet's presence
by the suitcase where he ran out of space
for the *h* of his name, or within

the carved frame of the cutlass chair
where he made sense of shifting days.
Later, they walk up the rocky garden
and a shadow falls across them
as they sit beneath his bower, taking stock.

De Quincey's Letter to Johnny Wordsworth 1809

He's taken such care to make it legible:
the faded copper ink neatly blocked,
a contrast to his *Confessions*, where words
are splashed on paper and blurred by winestains.

He promises to teach young Johnny
to sail across the lake, and walk on stilts,
lines curving slightly across the page
as if struggling to keep their balance.

Somehow, he found the space for this: to slow
his frantic pacing from room to room

and weave stories of his sailor brother
who spied on lions, bears and wolves,
hidden from giants in forests of eucalyptus,
and spent weeks on islands with no sun.

Halfway down the page there's a hole
made by the seal when the folds were opened.
There's a thought in there that's lost to us.
It's roughly the shape of a heart.

April in Town End

I wait for the clicking of cameras:
the cottage where the poet lived.
He complained of carts on cobbles
so what would he make of this, and us
who've built this shrine around him
and use these lanes like office corridors?
At Rydal Mount he greeted pilgrims
as his due so he may have enjoyed it,
even though his view of the unruffled lake
beneath the craggy folds of Silver Howe
is blocked by tall slate terraces
and tarmac slices through the valley.

Behind the Museum there's a grassy bowl
beside the steep slope of Dorothy's garden
where the noise from the road is dampened.
I read from *Home at Grasmere*
to the handful who've travelled
the cool darkness of the cottage parlour,
words he read to friends beside the fire.
Higher up, a slab of rock is planted,
rescued from blasts when Thirlmere was dammed:
WW, MH, JH, DW, JW, STC,
initials clear as yesterday.

Sheep at Night

This stone wall is often broken, through
heavy weather or motorists not knowing
the camber of the road. Sometimes a single
sheep wanders through the gap by accident,
galloping ahead of cars, their engines
whining, its fleece rising and falling
in panicked rhythm; or it trots in and out
of the trees opposite, bleating,
wondering what happened to its kin.

Tonight I'm the only driver, lakes and hills
slumbering in clouded moonlight.
At Rydal I round a bend, and there's
a flock of them, picking at tarmac.
Braking, I still must hit one, but strangely
they part around me. My headlights blur
their edges, create haloes around them.
Each is calmly itself in union
with others, and even from in here
I sense the special power of the herd.

Bowness: Early Morning

The Pleasure Boat is a huge mechanical fact
sharpening the focus of the early light
but it's sleeping soundless in the water.

The clean white boards and green trim
of the Booking Office are firmly shuttered,
the Coachpark beside it stretching out, empty.

A wafer of mist hangs low over
Windermere's dappled depths. Belle Isle
sits in green seclusion. Larch and spruce

blur the horizon, something Alpine
in the North of England. Where the two shores meet
the Langdales are layers of colour, igniting.

There's only the odd slam of a lorry door
or the squawk of a lone mallard to ruffle
the silence. Later, shutters will open

and visitors mass up the pier to claim
the lake, and the stillness is heightened
by this sense of things about to waken.

Training

I've latched a thirty foot black cotton line
to a two year old Dachshund, so he can
wander through Eggerslack Wood.
Large for his breed, long barreled-body
brindled like an Alsatian, he trots, paws splayed,
along root-knotted paths, legs muscled
like a sprinter, barely aware that I've dropped
the line. I shout *Stop!* into the sheltered stillness,
then crouch, tempt him back with tone and treat.

Some praise and off again. He keeps
to the track at first but he's bred
for badgers in the Black Forest,
and it only takes a rustle or scent
and he slips into the skin of some former self,
forcing a trail through meadowsweet
and wild garlic, his change in direction
almost soundless, nostrils blazing, tail lashing,
oblivious to my calls of *Walter! Walter!*

Grasmere Green: Summer Equinox

At the mid-point of the working day
I wander into the village, weighing my options.
After days of skies like slate, the blue shocks.
Tufts of cumulus drift across brushstrokes
of cirrus, and a breeze loosens the sun's heat.
Trees by the lake, full-crowned with leaf,
jostle like green clouds. Stock Lane is jammed
with walkers fixed on spots beyond the village,
and coach parties searching for whatever you do
in the Lake District when the weather improves.

I find a space on the low wall edging the Green,
benches and grass crowded with families.
Above College Street, Stone Arthur and Seat Sandal
hold this side of the valley together.
A few jackdaws sail in on the breeze, strut
like gangsters: incongruous on a bright day,
heralds of winter. They take their time,
wait for what is dropped, for what remains.
A dark cloud crosses over
with a chill like rain, tipping the balance.

Silencing the Bells

A church has waited in this valley
since Oswald built the first from an oak.
The bells sing its presence, sound the hour,
draw the congregation across the fells.

Before the nave a hook hangs down
from the ceiling's marquetry. They used to
fix a screen to this to hide the altar, declare
the space for market stalls or casual shelter.

We don't have a screen but a platform
puts the altar in shadow, focuses
the eye on poets and their secular prayers.
The bells would disturb this so we silence them.

It's simply a matter of tugging two cords
that drop through gaps in the belfry,
fastening them to bolts in the wall,

but as we reach the hour there's a tremble
in the air, almost beneath hearing,
as if they won't stay silent long.

Dusk in Lindale

By the time I'm home, the sun has slipped
behind Cartmel Fell and the sky holds
its last light in a sparkling grey wash.
The early dark forcing a different rhythm,

I walk the dog before day fades completely.
On the street the dusk is a shabby cloth
which parts as others, coming home,
emerge from shadows in our path.

The last houses shine like orange beacons,
small against impending night.
Cars purr around the bend, headlight beams
thrust out, the road left darker than before.

Woods run parallel to the path,
the slatted fence almost invisible
so the trees seem closer, pastel smudges
holding drums of darkness between them.

The dog stops, quivering, small legs
braced, scenting the loamy Autumn air,
tuned into a world that exists beside us,
beyond the tangle of nettles and brambles.

Further on, at Castle Head, a roe deer springs
over the field. Russet, it flickers
like a faint torch in the growing night
before being extinguished completely.

The Duddon Valley

After weeks of rain the valley is a swamp,
its floor shimmering scarlet, where grass
is starved of light. The paths have faded,
just one hard winter from wilderness.

Wordsworth loved this place. He came here
in old age, but in mist ghosting the slopes
he saw Coleridge, and others he'd outlived
and felt the earth begin to shrug him off.

We cross Red Beck and I almost slip
on rain-greased stones, the coldness
of the stream visible, like vapour,
as it crackles, clear, over cobbles.

Ahead, the valley walls are patched
with snow. My steps slide off
and I'm forced to take a different route.
Then the land tilts.

I'm still upright but sweat prickles my face
and my breath seems to hover
ahead of me, out of reach.
These spells are more frequent now.

My friend is focused on his own ascent,
out of sight around the ridge.
I lean against a rock until it passes,
then set off again, regain my rhythm.

Meathop Road: Autumn

Overnight, the year has shifted gear.
Birches and alders, high on the Fell top
are sprays of ochre that yesterday were green.

The sky is blue but recent rains have left
their mark, pooling in holes in the tarmac,
the roaring stream threatening to break its banks.

We expected this road to be quiet
but cyclists and dogwalkers have been drawn out
like us, the light changing our perspective.

Brambles straddle verges like wire; a field
of maize has gone to seed, kernels fragile
as dust, things stripped to fundamentals.

Back home, we will pare back and parcel up
the life we have made together, ready
for reassembly in a more permanent home.

On the embankment, beneath the railway
sleepers, rosehips, haws and fronds of bracken
are tangled together in a gentle fire.

Hampsfell

This is what I wanted for us: Hampsfell
on a blue Autumn day, strewn with tracks,
threads to pick up and follow: the grassy path
that skirts the knoll; a clamber up through gorse;
the dirt track by the drystone wall
that tries to tame this part of the Fell.

In the open the winds are cold but loose,
with currents of warmth in the spaces they leave.
Limestone bones break through where soil is thin.
At a peak, a cairn grows daily: the Old Way
where monks and merchants passed,
small stones to prove we've been here.

From up here we can see that Cartmel
is a settlement in a fir plantation.
Morecambe Bay curves around us, the sea
like silver cut into pools and rivers
against a sandy bed, and hidden beaches
are clearly visible. You turn to me and smile.

There are other Ways. The spine of the Fell runs
higher still but, for us, to be here is enough.

Fishing with Raymond Carver

He knew the course of rivers like the lines
on his own face: the pools where trout lurk,
the rocky runs where salmon shimmer.

He knew every path through the woods,
the shortest distance down through maples
and cedar, lugging gear with easy grace.

He knew the right bait, warming maggots
beneath his tongue as he'd watched his father do,
twisting hook to line with calloused fingers.

He wouldn't mock my left-handed knots
but watch with pale eyes, intervening
just before the tangle became irredeemable.

He'd show me how to cast
in a perfect arc, and we would relax
on the bank, wait for the floats to plummet.

I'd be comfortable with his silence
though sometimes I may suspect that he was
looking beyond the rushing waters.

Still, if the float bobbed, he'd jerk the rod
and play out line, knowing the exact moment
to reel in, and when he pulled the fish out

and it thrashed on the bank, drowning in air
he'd still it with a single blow
as if in apology.

Roslin Glen

The river lets out bursts of argument
like a heated meeting, but behind it
there's the deep bass reminder of traffic
in the distance. Screened by the valley sides
and the curtain of bamboo, we sometimes
forget we're not far from the road.

Down here the light is green, filtered
through bracken and rhododendrons,
mosses on the path glowing from within.
An oak barring the way has been sawn through,
two halves slid apart, the crown in the water,
a gap just large enough to walk through.

※

When the path turns and climbs upwards,
we stay with the river. Duck under
the crippled birch and wend through ferns
and you will see the deer track, a narrow band
of fallen leaves, gleaming amber, copper,
russet, maroon: leading the way through

the long polished blades of woodruff.
Tomorrow the track will have darkened
with rain, edges less defined where leaves
have been kicked by wind, barely discernible
from the rest of the wood's broken floor, but
for now it will take us beyond where we've been.

※

The trees hold their silence, mute as if waiting.
The call of a rook or a single shout
are hard to pinpoint from down here
among the spare winter ranks.

Beneath a holly there's a mess of feathers,
black quills and white down, evidence
of a struggle, possibly a pigeon plucked
from flight by a buzzard, but the trees aren't telling.

Where the track just holds its footing between
river and slope, a fallen spruce blocks the way,
twigs and branches flailing from the trunk
as if grasping at new possibilities.

✵

Here, where the banks are shallow, the river
resolves its arguments, glides on smoothly.
Beyond here, it doubles back, forming
a boundary, no way across, the bridge long gone:
it's confident enough to do what it likes,
memory carried in brackish waters.

At the bend there's the ruin of a cottage,
an outline, little more than foundations,
dark stone lit with moss, earth floor, two rooms
and a chimney, from where the barkless
trunk of a beech curves, pale
as a giant tusk, reaching upwards.

Hawthornden Castle

It began underground, Pictish echoes
held in sandstone caves where rebels
trained, slipping between shadows
on the wooded banks of the River Esk.

Later came the Tower, walls three feet thick
with arrow slits, a ragged drop of sheer rock
to the river's bend. It's still here, guarded
by rooks, grass growing from rough heights.

A Hall used the tower as cornerstone
but was destroyed, the stone foraged for
the present house. The ruins wall the Courtyard,
window frames like empty doorways,

wilted buddleia wending around the columns.
The Well is so deep you don't at first see
the water, rogue seeds rooted in the rock sides,
an odd splash reaching from a different time.

More layers have been added: a kitchen,
a further floor, making truth hard to find.
Even Drummond himself is difficult
to see: heartbroken recluse in his poems,

in the portrait he's a roguish laird.
His Seat above the river is double-sided
for each mood: one facing back to shelter,
one following the Esk with its babble of voices.

The Gift of Snow

We were waiting and last night it fell.
Snow outlines sycamore, birch and maple:
held in their branches and doubling each
crabbed finger, revealing their second selves.
An ash is so fine, it's hardly there:
a snow-ash, a trembling metamorphosis.

The river flows through, fast, coppery
ringing a new note, as though passing
through here is enough to be changed.
The half-moon of beach seems larger
where snow shrouds rocks and roots, hiding
boundaries where things begin and end.

Footprints and tracks are cast on the crisp lawn.
Each clump of grass is a white flower.
The dead fox still lies by the woods, russet
fur stippled white. Most scavengers
have ignored it but a pair of rooks land,
take what they can in this strange new world.

Passing
i.m. Jane Grounsell

In the Sunday quiet of this Tapas Bar,
hidden away on a connecting street,
you are the subject our words keep missing.

I'm changing trains, my first time here
since that day in the chapel when we tried
to smooth a balm on the wound of your passing.

Friends told of the way you splashed in puddles,
your shrew-like laugh, and the rainbow sweaters
you knitted, far too large for their wearers.

But we still have the vulgar fact that you've gone
far too soon. Your absence now is solid
and real as the empty chair at our skewed table.

You've left the three of us with our odd number
and we're feeling our way with bits of news,
searching for ways to be together without you.

Wearing Glasses

When you were seven, you saw the world
through the bottoms of bottles, in frames
so heavy they bruised your nose,
as you braved jeers on the road to school.
Teenage years were the age of fashion:
stars and triangles in scarlet and mauve,
but with a widowed mother and shopgirl's wage
horn-rims were the best you could manage.

Down the years your careful savings fell
through holes in our clothes, but at fifty
you treated yourself: polychromic
lenses, that changed with the light,
in lightweight frames the colour of honey.
A year later your retina tore, shattering vision
into fragments, and neither laser nor silicon
could restore definition. Now you hide
behind your glasses as they darken in the sun.

I'm almost the age you were then
and the muscles in my eyes that shift
the focus, for close work, are tiring.
Reading needs to be held at a distance
that's impractical, so I have them prescribed:
light gold frames, barely noticeable, but
there's a tender shock of family resemblance
as they bring out all that's shared between us.

Power

The last time the electricity failed,
we watched through the window in settling dusk
as vans rumbled into the field next door
and workers in yellow tunics gathered by
the telegraph pole like pilgrims. Floodlights,
like artificial moons, cast the grass
in a white sheen. One worker shimmied up, others
rapt beneath, mumbling what looked like prayers.
No sudden blaze, but as they pulled away
we felt the certainty of returning light.

Back in Yorkshire, during the strikes,
powercuts were balanced around districts.
With no television, we were forced
to talk to each other, while we played *Scrabble*
in the glow of candles, ignoring shadows
flickering around us, and when light
returned everything to its proper place
I ran to the window to watch
the small miracle of darkness
as it took over the estate below.

The Cottage

It marked the boundary between redbrick streets
and woods: thatch roof, stone gables, chimney
pluming with sweet smoke, white fence,
roses spilling over whatever the season:

an image from *Hansel and Gretel*, *Goldilocks*,
the family that lived there rarely glimpsed,
an occasional strain of a different
music teasing from an open window.

In time, avenues and streets reached out, houses
springing up on sports fields and scrubland,
around the chiselled face of the quarry,
woods pushed back by more brick terraces.

I heard that the cottage, empty
for over a decade, had been stolen
piece by piece: each stone, door and casement
removed by moonlight and carried away.

I doubt very much that this is true,
but I still like to imagine it rebuilt
beside an office block or in a carpark,
holding on to its small enchantment.

Message in a Bottle

While you shuffle around on the beach
an idea suddenly lights your face:
a slip of paper, slid inside a bottle,
name and address in brave red capitals,
announcing your presence to a distant shore.

You race to where the waves scribble on the sand
but the Captain of the waiting *Seal-Spotter*
stops you, offers to take the bottle out
to the open sea, away from this bay
where it will surely be scuppered by rocks.

Silently you search for courage to refuse.
Yesterday we took their trip, through mist
so thick we couldn't see the seals
gliding and playing in promised sunlight
just beyond the harbour's walls.

You prefer to place your faith
in the tiny strength of your own arm,
or at least in the pull of the waves
that submerge the bottle but seconds later
return it to the surface, carry it on.

Songlines

(1) The Rise and Fall of Ziggy Stardust

came through the ceiling one Sunday
while I had tea at Graeme's house. His brother
slipped among us like another visitor
from the stars, eating then returning
to the separate planet of his bedroom,
moving the stylus back to the beginning.

Drums, like an off-beat heart, gained strength
till the single crashing note heralded
Bowie telling us we only had
five years left to cry in. After that,
he was everywhere: body stretched ,
red and blue lightning on his face.

He invited us to follow him, leave behind
school, where we filed through corridors
in uniform ranks, at a bell's command;
the bus home crammed with faces
smeared black from coalmines or steel mills;
or the cul-de-sacs which blocked the light.

Years on, I found where they shot
the cover: not another land after all,
an alley just off Regent Street. I passed
beneath the *K West* sign, stood in the phonebox
suffused in orange from a streetlamp,
still ready to be taken to other worlds.

(2) Badlands
It's the working, the working, just the working life
    – Bruce Springsteen *Factory*

He was singing about New Jersey
not South Yorkshire, but cooling towers
smeared steam into our skies too. There was no
darkness on the edge of town, with no break
between towns chained together by factory lights.

There were no boardwalks to strut but Fridays
workers washed away the grime and dressed
to wring some pleasure from the working week.
Sixth formers, we stayed in corners, but George
was punched when someone didn't like his shirt.

We were promised an exit, to university,
and the music was my reason to believe:
his voice like a furnace; thundering pace
to burst through any barrier; words
that saw beyond these shortened days.

Neil and Cathy looked set for passage out
then she got pregnant, they got married
and he signed on at British Steel, not long
before it was broken up. I thought of them
when Bruce came on the radio. Unlike the song

no-one would have swum in our river
but I wonder if they ever drove out
to Ladybower to stare at the water
for a glimpse of the Church Steeple,
last sign of the drowned village.

(3) Seeing Bob Dylan with my Father

We take our seats in the Sheffield Arena.
I haven't seen you in over a year
but you still wear that permanent shrug
as if you couldn't have expected more
than your family, and a job packing bottles
that passes the days and pays the bills.

On rare days we had the house to ourselves
you'd slip LPs from the cupboard like secrets:
Highway 61 Revisited, The Freewheeling Bob Dylan.
racing rhythms or a simple guitar and voice,
that lifted us beyond the redbrick terrace
to candlelit bedsits and winter alleys.

This skeletal steeltown became a smudge
on my horizon, but I came back to bring you
here. Dylan plays like a man starting over,
and the words we share along with him
take the place of things we'll never say.

Leadburn

The Inn we stumbled across at a junction,
its restaurant in a railway carriage
projecting from the building, had that sense

of being between places, perfect
for slipping out of the city, and
a midpoint for friends when we moved out west.

A few days after I last sat in there
a passing truck driver dozed at the wheel,
climbing the pavement, razing the building.

All that remained was a fenced-off compound
with stray timbers and a few bricks
in a broken outline. Five years on

they've rebuilt it: smaller, two glass walls,
a deeper view of the Pentland Hills,
railway carriage gone:

the illusion of travel abandoned,
We've crossed the border now and we want it
to be our final stop but we're briefly back

and pop in to get our bearings as we pass.
A couple in the corner can't stop touching,
completely lost in the present.

Homecoming

One side of Dad's face has fallen
but his smile fights for purchase and just wins.
The effort to lift his hand in greeting
is almost visible, like static,
but fingers remain fixed on the sheet.

He's his own ventriloquist,
lips not moving as he speaks.
I lean in and a shadow dims his eyes.
I'm shut out while he watches
the private film his mind is running.

My brother drives me back to the station,
past the sites of demolished factories,
places where Dad found and lost himself.
The sky above us is cobalt blue but
I know I'll remember it washed out.

When I finally arrive in Grange-over-Sands,
the air off the bay is cool and liquid.
Just beyond the lights Amanda stands,
with Walter the dachshund, his yips
of greeting rising over the departing engine.